AUSTRIA

Gerhard Trumler · Johannes Sachslehner

AUSTRIA

DISCOVER · EXPERIENCE · REMEMBER

Pichler Verlag

CONTENTS

A COUNTRY
WITH DEPTH

Never have I boasted about my homeland
And loved it yet so much.
Conrad Ferdinand Meyer

Anybody who has ever looked for Austria whilst slowly turning a globe will know that Austria is not a large country. But it has a large history; its name has weight. Austria, "rich in honour and victories," has participated in the good and bad fate of Europe. It is a country in which paths of the peoples have crossed; a land of bloody disputes and fruitful coexistence. In numerous wars its infantrymen and soldiers killed and died; at congresses and conferences its diplomats bargained with countries and peoples; its artists and scholars created everlasting works. The victims of the battle fields are forgotten, the contracts and pacts of yesteryear have long crumbled into dust under the iron hand of time – yet the major cultural efforts of its geniuses will remain forever anchored in peoples' minds. This lively inheritance of its history and culture lifts the country up, enriches it. Not only rich in memories but also in places of remembrance, rich in unique treasures. In the mosaic of European cities from whose history Austria is inextricably connected, this "larger Austria" holds a particular place.

The poet Anton Wildgans once wanted to see the "custodian of the entire cultivated humanity" in Austria. His vision was a country that proudly administrated the "precious inventory" that left him a varied past. Without a doubt, Austria today scoops more than ever from this inheritance, cultivates and looks after its traditions and state-supporting narratives; even its world image nourishes itself on established myths, which are tirelessly and successfully restaged: the Habsburg dream couple Sisi and Emperor Franz Joseph and the drama surrounding their son Rudolf; the eternal music heroes Mozart,

Beethoven and Schubert; the cultural highlights the Burgtheater and Festspiele in Salzburg, culinary evergreens like the Wiener Schnitzel and Salzburger Nockerl and the attributed Austrian character traits such as their happy-go-lucky disposition and congeniality.

These are the favoured and familiar images of Austria as they are repeatedly presented. But this country is much more. It is worth looking behind the sleek façade of the much-trumpeted clichés. Those wanting to really get to know Austria shouldn't allow themselves to be blinded; they need to take the time to find out a few things about the country. Austria is more than the *Sound of Music* and Romy Schneider's *Sisi* films suggest: It isn't an enclave unchallenged by the spirit of modern dirndl-wearing girls and happy yodellers, speedy skiers and lederhosen-wearing hikers, not a blissful island of wine taverns and pub-romantics.

Even if the image of the Austrian abroad, not always without reason, is connected to a certain Alpine crankiness, to ruralness and retrocession – this country has very much arrived in the present. This is not least attributable to the difficult experiences encountered on its way into the 20th century; it has gained self-confidence and a sense of security. To a certain degree the country has learned to sum up its chances and possibilities as a small state. But this wasn't always the case: "The world is in turmoil but Austria is not going under," the writer and satirist Egon Friedell concluded easily even before 1938. In the meantime, Austria was destroyed, but rose again. The tough political reality doesn't hold to any clichés – and in the

Page 2: Known as a place of pilgrimage across borders: the pilgrimage church Unsere liebe Frau vom guten Rat in Hinterhornbach, district Reutte, Tyrol.
Previous page: A veritable garden of Eden: Klapotetz bei Ratsch in southern Styrian wine country.
Opposite page: A land of peace: View from the photographer's house in Langschlag, Waldviertel.

process, led the Austrian Jew Egon Friedell, who so desperately believed in Austria's invulnerability, to the grave. Following Austria's annexation to Nazi Germany, in order to avoid being arrested, Friedell jumped out of the third storey of his house and died.

And still in 1968, the year of the political unrest in Europe, the writer Hans Weigel wrote: "Austria doesn't know itself. Austria seeks its meaning in the past and future and has equally as many answers at the ready as there are Austrians – and Austria's meaning lies precisely in the multitude of conflicting answers to this question." Weigel's laconic conclusion to this finding: Austria is the "unification of those who cannot be unified," the "state embodying contradictions", the "overcoming of geography through history, the overcoming of politics through psychology."

As a matter of fact, the Republic of Austria, founded on 12 November 1918, fought long for this "meaning"; finding each other were only a few intellectuals, who became defenders of the young state and who also allowed it an idea and "mission". Among these few was the already mentioned Anton Wildgans, who in his "Speech on Austria" given in 1929 on the 11th anniversary of the republic, encouraged the development of an appropriate historical consciousness, the reflection of the particular culture of the "Austrian people" – desire that was only partly fulfilled, for the self-image of Austrians, the so-called "Austrian identity", remained disputed in the years of bloody conflicts between the parties. The new state, in Hitler's shadow under the federal chancellors Engelbert Dollfuß and Kurt Schuschnigg, which became an experimental field of anti-democratic power trips, counteracted the abyss.

In order to understand the Austrian dilemma in the context of its meaning-giving "state idea", it is necessary to look back even further. The Habsburg monarchy, an anti-modern political system, was an empire of old Europe, not a strictly organised central state but a confederation of countries and confraternity of peoples that had grown over centuries, held together by a major central principle: the dynasty. The land of the double-headed eagle was the classic "multiethnic state" and thus the last stronghold per se against the delusional ideas of nationalism. The English journalist Archibald Ross Colquhoun spoke of the "whirlpool of Europe". As reactionary, anachronistic and backwards as this state was in many ways, it was also moulded by the spirit of liberalism and a political cul-

ture, which focused on compromises and the balancing out of interests. It constituted a closed culture and economic realm in the heart of Europe, which offered its "small" nationalities protection from the greediness of the large nations – protection above all from the imperialism of the German Reich and tsarist Russia.

But it is a historical fact that not few Austrians fell into the hands of the nationalist, racial and ultimately fascist demagogues. Because of this, also Austrian writers felt obliged to render homage to a German nationalist cultural arrogance in the maelstrom of German imperialism – an arrogant attitude which attests to embarrassing ignorance, for the Danube monarchy was an alliance of nations whose members were thoroughly proud of their respective cultural merits. The propagandists of the "German spirit in Europe" didn't dispute this, however. They saw Austria-Hungary as a "powerful, independent bastion" against the barbarians of the East, as "scapegoats for the approaching anti-German bettors from the East" – a historical misrepresentation in which the Habsburgs consequently deteriorated into stuffy agents of "Germandom".

The judgement from littérateurs like Hugo von Hofmannsthal was a little more differentiated. Also he, the author of *Everyman*, staged each year in Salzburg, saw Austria-Hungary as a "borderland, rampart, termination" between the "European empire and an advancing, always chaotically-moving batch of people half-Europe, half-Asia", but admitted that not only was there a "cultural wave moving east-ward" but also a "westwardstriving counterwave", that was being "received". According to his essay published in December 1917 in the Neues Zürcher Zeitung, his summary of the "Austrian idea" stated that Austria's "only task and raison d'etre" was the downright fateful "equalisation with the East", the "equalisation of the ancient European Latin-Germanic with the new European Slavic world".

The "Ostmark thought" lived on in this way for decades before March 1938. The myth of the marginality of the country determined and penetrated not least also the debate about Austrian art, which on the one hand was described as being a "valuable and glittering gem in the crown of the German creative genius". This was according to the photographer Alois Schmiedbauer from Salzburg in his preface to his photographic book published in 1938 *Verborgene Schönheit. Bauwerk und Plastik der Ostmark – Hidden beauty. Construction and Sculp-*

View of the Schesaplana mountain in the Rätikon mountain range, Vorarlberg. This is the geological border between the Western and Eastern Alps.

"Enchanting valley" in the heart of Lower Austria: Dürnstein. The castle in which Richard Lionheart was once held captive was blown up by the Swedes in 1645.

ture of the Ostmark. It's no wonder that, in consistent execution of this way of thinking, the origins of "ost markian" art were declared "Nordic-Germanic" and individual regions of the country such as the Wienerwald were reinterpreted in mythological landscapes of ancient Germandom. One pictured Wotan riding through the forests of the "Ostmark" and the goddess of spring Ostara refreshing herself at the holy fountains; the fact that the Eastern Alps was a Celtic settlement area was obstinately suppressed for a long time.

The impression was even more drastic from the outside. In his much-read *Deutsche Schriften – German Writings* published in 1878, the anti-Semite Paul de Lagarde (1827–1891), a mastermind of German imperialism, maintained that Austria "long

doesn't have an existence principle". One didn't know why it existed; there was "no other role than for Austria to become a colonial city of Germany". The "non-German line of the Danube empire, the Magyars especially" were, according to Lagarde "simply an encumbrance for Europe: the faster they perish, the better for us and for them". Austria could only be kept, as was the conclusion of this virulent pan-German, by being "ruthlessly" Germanised.

Effectively, ideologists such as Lagarde only had limited understanding for the extremely fine threads that held the Habsburg monarchy together at heart. Above all, they preferred to underestimate the magnitude of the reverence shown to the dynasty and the monarchs. As the British journalist Henry Wickham

Steed commented even before World War I, the average citizen felt almost intuitively that the tyranny in the modern world wasn't threatened by monarchs, but from industry magnates, banks and interest-hungry investors. The monarch was thus even seen as a natural ally. And regarding Emperor Franz Joseph, his popularity and his prestige was not least due to the fact that it was never possible to link personal enrichment to the emperor's measures or deeds. Furthermore, Franz Joseph always had an eye on the needs of his "subjects". The crown, concluded "Wickum" Steed, an anti-Semite and German-hater, who paradoxically at the end of World War I would work on the destabilisation of Austria-Hungary in the secret Department of Propaganda in Enemy Countries at the Crewe House in London, was thus in no way dead ballast, in order to keep the balance, but an "active force", which consciously countered the excessive accumulation of social and political power.

However, the old monarch, the empire's major figure of integration, wasn't protected from misunderstandings surrounding his "Germandom". "Sir, I am a German prince!" Emperor Franz Joseph I declared to King Eduard VII – to thus call him the "Patriarch of the Anschluss", as the journalist Friedrich Heer once did, is wrong. Like so many of his subjects, the emperor, conscientious, modest and diligent, was dazzled by the full-bodied phrases of German nationalism. Franz Joseph and his ministers didn't know how to counter the pretentious rhetoric of "Germany, Germany above all!" Numerous members of German-national, all-German and folkish circles, fanatic Bismarck-admirers and anti-Semitic scatterbrains with their political views already stood outside the state realms of the Habsburg monarchy, which side by side with the German Reich, the "Nibelung faithful" "brother in arms", in the end sunk into decay.

The declaration of war against Serbia in July 1914, covered by the warranties of German generals for military assistance, represented the beginning of World War I for Austria-Hungary. Following desperate, murderous struggles at the fronts of Galicia, the Balkans, Isonzo and in the mountains of South Tyrol the multiethnic state collapsed at the heart of Europe; in autumn 1918 the German-speaking countries found themselves integrated in the German-Austria Republic from which the Republic of Austria emerged after the peace agreement of Saint-Germain 1919, a state that "no-one wanted" and which fought for survival from the very beginning. The goal of uniting all the German-speaking areas of the monarchy finally failed at the negotiations in the Parisian suburb. The outskirts of Bohemia and Moravia, parts of Tyrol, Carinthia and Styria had to be ceded to Czechoslovakia, Italy and Yugoslavia.

At the Saint Germain peace conference French president Georges Clemenceau is reported to have shouted "L'Autriche, c'est que reste! – Austria is what remains!" and with this cynical formula summed up the facts the way the victorious powers of World War I presented it: The new Austria, the republic, was simply the "rest" of a lost empire, an eighth of the only now existing Austria-Hungary with six-and-a-half million inhabitants. The orphaned core lands of the Habsburg Empire now saw that their task was to group themselves together in a new political system and to develop a new republican identity. They weren't given great chances: for many observers outside their borders, the new state structure was destined to fail and an imminent decline was forecast.

And what the new state "Germany-Austria", later only "Austria", was supposed to be was unclear to many of its citizens. Those who saw themselves as being members of the German cultural world and the German nation – among these many members of the highly educated elite – pulsated on the "annexation" to "humiliated" Germany, as decreed in the Versailles peace documents. Others dreamed of revolution, some of restoration. The agitators from the right, who rallied against the Jews, railed against the government and in their "Führer" Adolf Hitler saw the saviour, simply spoke of a "Drecksstaat – *dirty state*". The explanation given by "Federal Chancellor" Karl Renner on 12 November 1918, Proclamation Day, in front of the provisional National Assembly was indicative of the confusion that reigned over the new identity of the new state. He spoke of "our German folk", of "origins" and a "mutual fate". To the approval of the loud applause of the members of parliament, Renner thus formulated a mortgage that burdened the young state from its inception onwards.

The fatal "German" perspective and the growing anti-Semitism consequently hindered the clear delineation from German fascism, the Christian Socialist's party programme from November 1926 explicitly demanded "fostering the German way" and the fight against the "superiority of the corrosive Jewish influence on intellectual and economic areas". The "arrangement of the relationship to the German empire" was to be based on the right of self-determination of the people. In a disastrous way, this is how the broad circles of the Austrian political elite paved the way for National Socialism. Infused with German national, racist and anti-Semitic slogans, following the Anschluss, no small number of Austrians are prepared, in the name of the Führer, whom they enthusiastically received, to murder. The Holocaust is decidedly borne by perpetrators from Austria. With their harrowing murders, men like Adolf Eichmann, Odilo Globocnik, Ernst Kaltenbrunner and Amon Leopold Göth were able to rely on the silent "blind eye" of many; their advantage having been the extensive lack of a conscience, which identified the crimes as wrong. Austrian society cannot be acquitted of its complicity in the Nazi crimes – at least not across the board.

The volition of the victorious powers reconstructed an independent and democratic Austria in 1945. The Moscow Declaration of 30 October 1943 recognised that Austria was the first country to have fallen victim to the "typical aggression politics of Hitler" and thus had to be freed of National Socialist role. Austria's joint responsibility in the participation of the war at Hitler-Germany's side in no way went without mention by the Allies. After 1945, however, this point was all too preferred to be suppressed; the victim stance was taken and the "final reckoning" with National Socialism demanded by the Allies was neglected. And thus the honest "soul searching" which was necessary to make peace with National Socialism, remained unacknowledged. Numerous officials and officers of the Nazi regime were able to continue their careers in the Second Republic unchallenged. The restitution of Jewish assets dragged on and the persecution of the murderers was only done half-heartedly. It was left to the private initiative of a Simon Wiesenthal to track down a man like the Holocaust mastermind Adolf Eichmann. And precisely this half-heartedness in dealing with his own past was the downfall of President Kurt Waldheim, who had to pay dearly for this failure.

The once-loved and popular notion *Heimat – homeland* in the meantime also finally became a loaded concept. The Austrian writer Robert Menasse (born 1954) in his comments about Austrian identity rightly repeats that the idea of *Heimat* was destroyed by the Nazis. Using "continued profitable transformation", the goal was to turn the Heimat into an "ensemble of backdrops". A finding that mainly rests on the images that the Austria's "anti-heimat literature" portrays: here, in the works of Thomas Bernhard, Peter Turrini, Josef Winkler or Peter Handke, it is about a country in which one can no longer feel "at home". Austria is a "nation without heimat", the "anti-heimat par excellence", branded by "false idylls" and "murderous clichés". According to Menasse's critique, Austria has "sold out" to the tourists, a "deserted ensemble of art and natural beauty" has been produced while the Austrians themselves have flown from "ideological transvestism" and the "folkloristic theatre of the folk of publicans and hosts", whereby at the same time a "mental continuity" from the Nazi time by all means still exists. Anyone who knows modern Austria knows the reproach that Austrians have given up themselves through their "radical surrender" to tourism and transformed the country into a "recreation area and museum" in this polemic exaggeration is not true. Above all, the development towards mass tourism is not new and also has nothing to do with ideology. Since the Biedermeier era, the view to the landscape in Europe has changed. Natural wonders and monuments of the past are visited in order to admire them and to let one self go. The business of "sightseeing" is as old as the term itself.

The phenomenon of mass tourism definitely has a new dynamic – it used to mean closing one's eyes to reality if one wanted to overlook that regions and cities, individual sights and tourist offers had to prove themselves in the constant state of competitiveness today. For a long time now, each community, each city, tries to make their attractions as competitive as possible. Perhaps Hans Magnus Enzensberger was right in his critique by saying that the "freedom from the industrial world" aspired to through tourists has long since established itself as an industry and the "journey from the consumer world" has become a commodity itself. Yet a retreat from the commodity "tourism" would be an illusion for Austria. The country would suffer a major economic crisis.

In the meantime the number of Austrian citizens who now see Austria as one nation has risen: at the end of the 1950s it was about 50 per cent of Austrians; in 2004 according to a survey, about 76 per cent. The idea of belonging to the "German folk", which caused confusion for so long, hardly plays a role any more – if you ignore the fanatic right-wing extremist individuals like the "letter bomber" Franz Fuchs, who between the years 1993 and 1995 caused unrest with his series of letter bombs. What is certain is this: The political identity of modern Austria is no longer connected to the bloodthirsty deity of "nationalism". In the reflection of its inheritance – even if not

Traditions lovingly upheld: An accordion player at a must wine tavern in Ybbsitz *(above left)*; Salting the wheel of cheese in a cheese dairy in Salzburg *(above right)*; Corpus Christi procession in Wurmbrand, Groß Gerungs, Lower Austria *(below)*.

Above: A charming sport city known world wide: Kitzbühel with St. Andrew's church and the Liebfrauenkirche.
Opposite page: The Riesenrad: Standing 65 metres high, it has been inviting guests to rides through the ether for over one hundred years in the Vienna Prater.

totally overcome in all areas – its citizens have recognised that they can be patriotic without beating their drums; that enemies have become friends and that it's about building a future together. And even if the politics of the European Union, of which Austria has been a member since 1 January 1995, is sometimes seen with scepticism, and some decisions from Brussels are critically received, even if the results of the politics of the day often only trigger sullenness and critique and one doesn't want to have anything to do with the politicians "up there" – the basic democratic orientation of the Austrians is beyond all question; freedom, human dignity and democracy are values for which the majority of population would also be willing to fight should a threat occur. Austrians have found their state, acknowledged it and accepted it; they have taken the important step that, according to French historian Jules Michelet formulated back in 1848, is necessary in order to be able to feel at home in their home country, their homeland, to reach the "universal fatherland".

leupolt der tugenderich

THE BECOMING
OF A NATION

The region that is now contained within the borders of Austria was shrouded in foreign barbarism for geographers of the antiquity. The land of vast forests behind the snow-covered Alps, traversed by a large river only slowly came into the focus of occidental consciousness. And this although the Alp-Danube region was a hub for foreign trade: salt from Hallstatt and Hallein, iron from the mining regions in Carinthia and gold from the Hohe Tauern mountains were sought-after goods; Bernstein Strasse, which ran along the eastern side of the Alps, saw the transport of the coveted gold-yellow gemstone from the Baltic Sea coast to the south. Even the conquering and occupation of the Celtic region to the Danube by the Romans under Emperor Augustus around 15 BC didn't change much about the peripheral position of the region. For the Romans the newly defined Danube provinces of the 1st century AD – Rhaetia, Noricum and Pannonia – represented borderland exposed to attacks from the German peoples, about which little is written. With their characteristic diligence, the Roman provincial administration developed the land. A dense network of roads was built, Celtic and Rhaetian settlements not destroyed by war became oppida, small municipal communities; emerging villages like Brigantium (Bregenz), Aguntum (near Lienz), Lentia (Linz), Vindobona (Vienna), Virunum (am Zollfeld in Carinthia), Flavia Solva (Wagna bei Leibnitz), Cetium (St. Pölten), Lauriacum (Enns), Ovilava (Wels) and Juvavum (Salzburg) were chartered during Roman rule; the legion camp Carnuntum between Deutsch-Altenburg and Petronell became the main military base of the Roman Empire on the Danube.

The ordered Roman world on the Danube in which Christianity had long found foothold sank under the influx of peoples from the north and east; Germanic tribes and Slavs, Huns and Avars found a new settlement area here. Some of the Roman villages remained, however, and were expanded by the settlers and built up into fixed locations. In around 800 at the eastern border of the Frankish Empire under Charles the Great, who destroyed the Avar empire in bloody wars, borderlands were developed, the Friaul March in the south and the Avar March on the Danube, the first new administrative units that marked the beginning of the governmental independence of the territories that Austria would later emerge from. But it was a long road. One century later, the rule of the Carolingians ended, the Avar March was overrun by the Hungarians. It wasn't until the defeat of a Hungarian mounted cavalry in 955 in the battle of Lechfeld that the eastern frontiers were eventually won back again.

The year 976, as Emperor Otto II enfeoffed the "March on the Danube" to Count Liutpold (Leopold I) of the Babenberg dynasty – in the same year Carinthia became a dukedom – marks the beginning of the expansion and thus the final rise of the "Ostland". Margrave Liutpold moved his residence from Pöchlarn to Melk as early as 984; around 1045 Tulln became the capital city. In the meantime, the Babenberg margraves moved their borders up to Thaya, March and Leitha. Around 1113 Leopold III, the Holy, moved his residence in Klosterneuburg; in 1158 Henry Jasomirgott eventually made Vienna a capital city, and from this point onwards, the fate of the country was decided from here.

In the meantime the Babenbergs had also advanced to duke status: in the "Privilegium minus" of 1156 King Friedrich I Barbarossa proclaimed Austria a duchy. Only four decades later, in 1192, did Styria fall to the Babenbergs due to the legal line of succession according to the Georgenberg Pact of 1186.

Opposite page: Legendary origins of the Austrian coat of arms: Emperor Frederick I Barbarossa handing over the new red-white-red flag to Count Leopold V the Virtuous, after the battle of Akkon. Detail from the Babenberg family tree in Klosterneuburg Abbey.

Terra Austria (a term first used in 1136) thus became a power on the Eastern flanks of the Holy Roman Empire in its own right. At this point in time, the German appellation for the land of the Babenbergs had already been established. A document of Emperor Otto III, dated 1 November 996, the name "Austria" or Ostarrîchi (from Old High German Ôstarrîhhi), was used for the first time. It literally means "eastern empire", whereby "reich" is used in the sense of "domain" or "territory". In this document Emperor Otto III bestowed the Bishopric of Freising in Bavaria with a court with attached land that was situated in Neuhofen an der Ybbs in today's western Lower Austria. The term Austria used in the Latin texts may sound Latin but its origins are the Old German *austar-, Old High German ôstar- "eastern, in the east", from which the Latin term Austria eventually came. And thus in 1147, in a document of King Conrad III, the margraves of Austria are referred to as *Austrie marchionibus*.

The Austrian sovereigns rose to respected and influential noblemen; their court in Vienna was one of the most important and glamorous residencies in the German lands. In the 13th century, however, a dramatic change occurred at the top of the dukedom: The 270-year rule of the Babenbergs ended in 1246 when Duke Frederick the Quarrelsome fell in 1246 at the battle against the Hungarians by the Leitha river; the fight for the coveted inheritance became a decade-long struggle. In 1278 King Rudolf von Habsburg emerged victorious over his great adversary, the King of Bohemia Przemysl Ottokar II, in the battle at Weidenbach between Dürnkrut and Jedenspeigen. The Habsburgs then rose to power in the former Babenberg countries. In 1282 King Rudolf invested his sons Albrecht and Rudolf with the dukedoms of Austria and Styria. The newcomers from the west might not have been liked, but they new how to cleverly increase their power base to eventually create a world-encompassing empire in which the sun never set. From the onset, their complex of territories grew swiftly: in 1335 Carinthia fell to Austria, in 1363 Tyrol; in 1375 the Habsburgs acquired the county of Montfort (Feldkirch and inner Bregenz Forest) in Vorarlberg.

The ascension to the most powerful territorial state of the empire in the late Middle Ages also saw the development of the landscape. Castles and newly-founded cities sprang up, diligent colonialists created new farmland by clearing the vast forests; improved farming implements and new technologies increased revenues for the farmers and thus also increased the population. Foreign trade blossomed and opened the scope for the foreign and the exotic. At the same time the identification with the country intensified. The inhabitants of the Austrian countries on the Danube called themselves Osterman, Austrians. Salzpurgaere, Stiraer and Kernaer were proud of their homeland; their aspiring cities gave evidence of power and opulence, trade and security; self-confident citizens, the *cives*, drawing on their documented privileges, increased their political influence and confronted landlords of the territory as autocratic trading stakeholders.

The most important founding of a town in the Late Middle Ages was that of Wiener Neustadt, which became an important fortification in a period of only a few centuries. The nobility also founded numerous cities; Zwettl, Weitra, Gmünd, Dürnstein and Zistersdorf exist thanks to the Kuenringer dynasty; in the West, Innsbruck (first mentioned in a document in 1187), was chosen by the powerful counts of Andech, who made it their centre of power; in Bregenz, the former Roman naval port Brigantium, the hardly less influential Count of Montfort ruled and on the remains of the ancient Roman city Iuvavum the prince archbishop's residence Salzburg was built.

Graz, today the second-largest city in Austria, was first mentioned as early as 1128/29; in 1379 it became the residence of the Leopoldine line of the Habsburgs. In 1252, Klagenfurt, later to become the capital city of Carinthia, received a town charter. Ten years earlier, in 1242, the East Tyrol capital Lienz is referred to as a city. The oldest still preserved municipal law document is the one from Enns and originated in the year 1212. Even earlier, in 1159, the Lower Austrian capital city St. Pölten received town status.

The mobility of individual parts of the population grew; merchants and trades people were on the move; caravans pulled by pack animals travelled the roads, pilgrims, couriers and beggars wandered from village to village. Where possible, ships sailed the waters. Hospices were erected on mountain roads for travellers, the first bridges made water-crossing possible. From this point onwards, ordered traffic and communication structures defined the landscape; cities and markets, castles and monasteries interacted with each other. Slowly the conviction spread that the country 'existed' united.

Inextricably tied to the becoming of the nation was the huge influence of the church. As the castles and cities grew, so did the number of parishes and churches. Powerful monuments to

Above left: Cult figurines from the early Palaeolithic era: The famous Venus of Willendorf was created around 25,000 BC and can be seen in the Natural History Museum in Vienna.
Above right: Woman with Noric fur hat: Grave of the Celt Umma, Heimatmuseum Mannersdorf am Leithagebirge.
Below left: Roman gravestone from Flavia Solva, walled in in the outer wall of Seggau Castle, Styria.
Below right: Idol from the Neolithic period: Venus of Eggendorf, Höbarthmuseum Horn.

God, convents and monasteries, were built and announced the power of Governor God on earth. For example, the mighty Benedictines, whose origins in Melk fall during the time of the first Babenberg margrave Leopold I and who moved into their monastery in 1089 on the hill over the Danube. The proud Baroque house of God still greets visitors today.

The monks of the oldest monastery in Austria and the German-speaking realm also live according to the Benedictine principles in St. Peter's monastery in Salzburg, which was founded in 696 by St. Rupert and probably dates back to the monk society of the late Antiquity. Older than Melk is also Kremsmünster Abbey, which was founded in the year 777 by Bavarian duke Tassilo III. In around 1070 the Benedictine monks founded Millstatt Abbey in Carinthia; in 1091 the first Benedictine monks settled in the new St. Paul Abbey in the Lavanttal Valley. In 1094 they overtook Göttweig Abbey founded by the canons. In 1158 Benedictines of Irish descent founded the Schotten-kloster in Vienna.

The 12th century then saw the rise of the reform order of the Cistercians: the important abbeys Rein (1129), Heiligenkreuz (1133), Zwettl (1138) and Lilienfeld (1202) follow in quick succession. In 1272 Stams in Tyrol also followed. As well as the Cistercians, the Augustine canons, last but not least, catered for the expansion of the monastic community. In 1114 Margrave Leopold founded Klosterneuburg Abbey. In 1140 a Styrian nobleman founded the Seckau abbey; in 1163 Vorau Abbey was founded in the "Joglland" in Styria. In 1153 the reformed canons, the Premonstratensians, gained foothold by founding Geras Abbey in the Waldviertel. In 1218 they are also successful in the Upper Austrian town of Schlägl in the Mühlviertel.

A clever marriage policy paved the way for the house of Habsburg. In this way Emperor Maximilian I arranged his most spectacular coup in 1515. His grandchildren, Ferdinand and Maria, married Anna and Ludwig respectively in a double wedding in Vienna's St. Stephen's cathedral, the children of King Vladislas II of Bohemia and Hungary. Vladislas II died in 1516; his son Louis became king of Hungary but was killed in 1526 during the battle of the Mohács against the Turks. Because there was no progeny, the agreed contract of inheritance meant that Bohemia and Hungary went to the House of Habsburg, which thus then became the most powerful dynasty in Europe. Following protracted conflicts and battles, the Habsburg rulers were finally able to also assert themselves against Lutheranism and consolidate their position of power: their countries remained Catholic.

The memorable victory over the Turks in 1683 before Vienna and the ensuing successful offensive against the Ottoman Empire indicate the end of the "Turkish troubles"; the borders of the empire extended further to the south with the victorious battles of Prince Eugene of Savoy. Yet the multiethnic state of the Habsburgs was soon on the defensive again, wavering precariously under the battles against Frederick the Great and Napoleon. It never withstood the Revolution of 1848 and in 1859/1866 had to concede the loss of its Italian territories before sliding into the war of 1914, which would bring about the decline of the dynasty.

With the loss of the Habsburg lands in the East and South East, Austria moved "closer" to the Eastern Alps. The phrase "Alpine Republic" was coined and became an accepted metaphor for a country that was dominated by mountains: 52,600 km², that means 62.8 % of the country (83,871 km²), are mountainous. Tyrol alone has 640 mountain peaks higher than 3,000 metres. The world of mountains became the Austrian "energy arena" par excellence, the opening for tourism becoming the country's primary task.

The poet Wilhelm Szabo talked about the "blissful harmony of art, nature and history," which distinguished one of the most famous landscapes in Austria, the "enchanting piece of valley", the Wachau. "Where," he asks, "does one find the noblest, choicest, in such abundance collected in such a small area, images of nature and of people becoming, the exceptionally gifted hand of the artist, at the same time united with the solid witnesses and remains of a long lost knightly past?" A question that can be applied to the entire Austrian landscape with a clear conscience: Magnificent impressions not only exist between the houses of God between Melk and Göttweig; "The magical" is ubiquitous between Bodensee and Seewinkel in Burgenland, between the grey granite boulders of the Waldviertel Blockheide and the wildly romantic gorges and flumes in Carinthia. Those taking the time for an immediate, intensive encounter with the Austrian world will notice that it's worth it for the soul and body.

Opposite page: Witness to early Christendom in Austria: Chapel of St. Gertrude in the catacombs of the archabbey cemetery St. Peter, Salzburg.

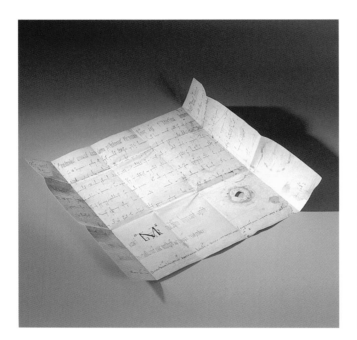

Above left: Documents the oldest known written use if the name "Austria": the Ostarrichi Document from 1 November 996. Bavarian State Archives in Munich.
Above right: Created in the 9th century from the gravestone of an inhabitant of the Roman city Virunum: the Carinthian duke's throne on the Zollfeld Plains.
Below left: Roman carriage. Stone relief on the other wall of the Maria Saal Cathedral in Carinthia.
Below right: Precious relic from the 8th century: The Tassilo chalice, donated by Bavarian Duke Tassilo, founder of the Benedictine Kremsmünster Abbey.

The most famous Roman monument in Austria: the Heidentor in Petronell-Carnuntum, a triumphal monument for Emperor Constantius II.

Above: In the crypt of the inner Benedictine monastery Nonnberg in Salzburg. The ribbed vaulting encompassing 18 columns originates from the late-Gothic era.

Opposite page
Above: From the six-storey keep of the Schauenstein castle ruins is a wonderful view of the Kamp river near Pölla.
Below left: "Pagan" demonism in Christian surroundings: Column embellishment in the Benedictine Millstatt Abbey, Carinthia.
Below right: St. Augustine. Fresco from the mid 12th century under the nuns' choir in the Nonnberg Abbey church.

Above: According to legend, this is where the loyal servant Blondel finally found his master, Richard Lionheart: Dürnstein, castle filled with history of the Kuenringers.
Opposite page: Still a sanctuary from the Turks in 1683: the old Babenberg castle Starhemberg, once generously enlarged by Duke Frederick II the Quarrelsome.

Schloss Schwertberg on the Aist, Upper Austria, formerly the seat of the robber-baron Bernhard Zeller, who was beheaded by the citizens of Linz in 1521.

Above left: Surveying the east Styrian hills from steep volcanic rock: what is known as the indomitable Burg Riegersburg.
Above right: The former castle St. Peter-Freienstein on the Styrian iron street was rebuilt by the Jesuits in to a church (Maria of Seven Sorrows).
Below left: Ancient weir system not far from Spitz an der Donau: the Hinterhaus ruins, once the administrative seat of the Kuenringers.
Below right: Burg Lockenhaus in Burgenland, seat of the infamous "Blood Countess" Elisabeth Báthory-Nádasdy.

Above left: At one with nature: St. Nikolaus parish church in Damüls in the Bregenz Forest.
Above right: Gothic church on a green pasture: St. Nicolas "in the peat bog" in Obertilliach, East Tyrol.
Below left: Romanesque jewel in Carinthia: the Gurk Cathedral. Its towers with two Baroque onion domes.
Below right: Famous for its magnificent Romanesque frescoes: St. Nicolas chapel in Matrei, East Tyrol.
Opposite page: Classic Gothic at 1300 metres above sea level: the church St. Vinzenz in Heiligenblut, behind it the powerful massiv of the Großglockner.

Above: Wine paradise in the heart of the Wachau: Spitz an der Donau with the Tausendeimerberg mountain. On the far left the Hinterhaus ruins.

Opposite page
Below left: Spruce blossoms in the Waldviertel: Green veils blow across fields and meadows.
Below right: The return of silence: Former Hammer *"In der Noth"* in Prollingbach bei Ybbsitz, Lower Austrian Eisenwurzen.

Rushing water: Höllfall, a cataract hundreds of metres long in the large Kamp river in Pretrobruck in the Waldviertel.

Breath-taking natural power: the Krimmler waterfalls in the Hoher Tauern mountains. With a falling distance of 380 metres, it is the fifth-largest waterfall in the world.

Above: Majestic mountain landscape shrouded in myths and legends: the Patteriol in the Verwall mountains, Tyrol, with one of its small, ice-blue lakes.

Opposite page
Above: Sunset over the Toten Gebirge mountains.
Below left: Nature reserve and Eldorado for sport climbers: the Wilde Kaiser mountain in Going.
Below right: Divers love its crystal-clear water: the Plansee Lake in the middle of the Lechtal Alps, the second-largest lake in Tyrol.
Following double page: A favourite destination: the Große Pyhrgas (2244 m), the highest plateau of the so-called "Haller Mauern" in the Ennstal Alps.

TREASURY
OF EUROPE

With the Habsburg monarchy's declaration of war on the kingdom of Serbia on 28 July 1914, the days of Old Europe were numbered. The catastrophe of World War I pulled the seemingly stable order of the continent into the abyss. On Ballhausplatz in Vienna the man responsible for the Austrian-Hungarian leadership, Foreign Minister Leopold Graf Berchtold and Chief of Staff Franz Conrad von Hötzendorf, lacked the resolve and ultimately also the will to avoid war. Fighting at the flanks of the German Empire, surrounded by military and materially superior enemies, the Habsburg Empire headed towards collapse. In autumn 1918 the imperial and royal armies reached the end of their strengths; on November 11, 1918, a memorable event occurred in Schloss Schönbrunn: Emperor Charles I declared that he "renounced participation" in state affairs and that he would recognize every decision made by the future form of government. The end of the Habsburg rule had come. On the night of the November 11, 1918, the royal family left Schönbrunn and withdrew from Vienna, moving east to Schloss Eckartsau. On 24 March 1919, just 641 years after the battle of Dürnkrut and Jedenspeigen, Charles I finally left Austria and sought asylum in Switzerland. The emperor, the "epitome of power of all empires, the symbol of Austrian endurance," according to Stefan Zweig in his memoirs *Die Welt von Gestern – The World of Yesterday* – lay in the past. And the writer Hans Weigel noted aptly: "In 1918 the Germans lost the war; we lost a world."

The royal family may have left Austria, but their castles, palaces and country estates, properties, which belonged to the so-called "courtly estate" and now became the property of the Republic or the other successor states of the Danube monarchy. The personal assets of the ruling family were impounded; the private court institutes of the emperor such as the Spanish Riding School, the court opera and the Hofburg theatre were passed over to the administration of the Republic. For the young state these "core pieces" of Old Austria were important elements for the creation of a new cultural identity. Going beyond all political trenches, the Burgtheater and Staatsoper communicated common ground; the former stages of the emperor now honoured the Republic, and from the cultural corner stones of the Habsburg Empire the foundations for the new Austria grew; previous reservations were overcome.

With the rule of the double-headed eagle now behind it, Austria was still obligated to the cultural heritage of the "black-yellow" state. It fed abundantly on the altercation with the ambiguous world of the perishing "Kakanien – imperial and royals", as Robert Musil and Joseph Roth describe so impressively in their works. Emerging from the feudal lifestyles of the once powerful were museums, attractions and sights, true treasuries of occidental cultural history. Locations of power that once were turned into nostalgically transfigured places of remembrance: Schloss Schönbrunn and the Hofburg, for example, the bright, magnificent summer palace on the edge of the residence and the house of the emperor, which had grown over centuries, as vast as it was labyrinthine at the entrance to the inner city of Vienna.

Who wouldn't feel the magic of a bygone era when looking at the exquisitely outfitted state rooms of Schönbrunn? Those who have walked the gravelled paths through the vast palace park, past the silver Neptune Fountain up to the Gloriette, the heroes' monument to the Habsburg armies and who have "absorbed" the entire beauty of the palace complex with all their senses will be able to imagine the glamour of the old monarchy, the magic of a place from which at one time the fate of an empire was decided.

Opposite page: A grand space for books: the largest monastic library room in the world in the Admont Benedictine monastery.

The visitor to the Hofburg may also be able to tap into the sounds of a distant past when entering the former chambers of the royal family. Unique rooms of remembrance, a world of conglomerated memories filled with the spirit of feudal Europe that here has one of its large, secret central points. The Treasury houses the insignias of the ancient empire, power symbols of a long-lost world: the crown of Holy Roman Empire and the Austrian imperial crown, the treasure of the Burgundians and the Order of the Golden Fleece. Jewels before which at one time citizens and patrons bowed, and which also represented hope. Hope for a wise and just ruler.

Imperial ancient Austria, however does not only exist in Schönbrunn and the Hofburg, in the Tyrolean Schloss Ambras and in the Capuchin crypt. It lives on in the Austrian Baroque. Born of the feeling of triumph of the victory over the Protestants and the Turkish "arch enemy", of the joy of having survived the major plague epidemics of 1679 and 1713, it is a veritable glittering reflection of occidental power of creativity. The "Baroque transformation" of Austria from that time, created by architects and engineers, by poets, preachers and composers from all over Europe, still defines the country today.

Experiencing Austria with open eyes means seeing that small Austria is still a giant, impressive Baroque stage honouring God and the emperor. Palaces and castles, domes, churches and monasteries are just as much a part of this art world where ancient stylistic elements and Catholic-imperial majesty, sensuality and lust for life are connected in a splendid way. Monumental houses of God such as the Benedictine abbeys in Melk and Göttweig, in Kremsmünster and St. Florian, magnificent structures like the National Library, formerly the court library, which celebrates Charles VI as the Roman emperor and ruler of heaven and earth, and the castles of Prince Eugene, above all the magical complex of the Belvedere Palace in Vienna, announce the magnificence and power of Old Europe and at the same time represent Austrian identity: shaped by open joviality, they bear witness to the character of this country and its people.

Right: Baroque central-plan building full of beauty and harmony: Karlskirche in Vienna, built between 1716 and 1739 by Johann Bernhard Fischer von Erlach.

Above: Unique Romanesque relief embellishment: The "stony bible" on the façade of the parish church Schöngrabern, Lower Austria, tells of the fight between good and evil.
Below left: Image documents from a distant era: fresco depictions of Pope Gregory, mid 12th century, Benedictine monastery Nonnberg, Salzburg.
Below right: The king of kings. Romanesque fresco in the former west choir of the church Lambach, Upper Austria.
Opposite page: Most likely a meeting point of early Christians: the Maximus chapel in the catacombs of the cemetery of the archabbey St. Peter in Salzburg.

Above left: The roof with the "pagan towers"; on the right, the southern tower – at 137 metres, one of Europe's tallest church towers.
Above right: Late Gothic plastic of unrivalled ease and power of expression: pulpit with the "window watcher", a self-portrait of the artist.
Below: In the vast innards of the cathedral: Mighty bundle pillars, decorated with six stone figures each, seem to rise endlessly.
Opposite page: Visible from afar, the emblem of Vienna and symbol of free, independent Austria: St. Stephen's cathedral.

Above left: A place of silence: the Gothic fountain house in the cloister of the Cistercian monastery in Zwettl in the Waldviertel.
Above right: Divine symphony of colours and forms: the insides of the Melk Abbey church with ceiling frescos by Michael Rottmayr.
Below left: Bright Baroque monastery landscape: the arcaded courtyard of the Cistercian monastery Heiligenkreuz in the Wienerwald.
Below right: The fountain house at Heiligenkreuz Abbey with impressive stained-glass windows.

Opposite page: Grand Baroque monastic palace on the Danube and corner stone of the UNESCO world cultural heritage Wachau: the Benedictine Melk Abbey.

Above left: Baroque "one-tower façade": the 90-metre tower of the Zwettl Abbey church.
Above right: In the oldest still existing monastery of the Cistercians: the library of Rein Abbey with its famous calendar table by Andreas Plenninger.
Below left: Stylish ambience: the Paulus room in the prelature of Geras Abbey.
Below right: Reflection of a Baroque attitude to life: the Augustine Reichersberg Monastery with the Michaelsbrunnen Fountain.

The herb garden of the Premonstratensian Geras Abbey with the abbey church Mariä Geburt.

Above: Imposing Austrian Monte Cassino over the valley of the Danube: The Benedictine abbey Göttweig.
Below left: The mighty west façade of the Augustine St. Florian monastery with the convent building and the church.
Below right: Its castle-like stature rules over the Oberinntal valley: the Cistercian Stams Abbey.
Opposite page: The second-largest Baroque staircase in Europe: the *Kaiserstiege* in the Göttweig abbey with a huge fresco by Paul Troger.

Above: Baroque temple of awareness: the Benedictine abbey Altenburg library, created by builder Josef Munggenast and painter Paul Troger.

Opposite page
Above: The huge library in St. Florian Abbey, spanned by a ceiling painting by Bartolomeo Altomonte.
Below left: Artistically worked gallery: the library of the Schlägl Premonstratensian monastery in the Mühlviertel.
Below right: Book treasury in Zwettl Abbey: The "Bärenhaut", a poem from the 13th century tells tales about the noble family Kuenringer.

Above left: A masterpiece by sculptor Meinrad Guggenbichler: the suffering saviour in the church in St. Wolfgang.
Above right: Lively features carved in limewood: St. Christopher. Detail from the Kefermarkt Altar, Kefermarkt church in the Mühlviertel.
Below left: Knight's battle with the lion: sculpture at the foot of the pulpit stairs in the Franciscan church Salzburg.
Below right: The "Escape to Egypt" with the first view of Vienna: Gothic panel painting by the "Scottish master" (mid 15th century), Benedictine abbey Our Dear Lady to the Scots, Vienna.

Opposite page: Life-size figures in stone pine: the winged altar by the South Tyrolean painter and carver Michael Pacher in the St. Wolfgang church in the Salzkammergut.

Above: Jewel form the Renaissance period: the magnificently painted inner courtyard of Schloss Tratzberg bei Jenbach in the Tyrolean lowlands.

Opposite page
Above left: Famous for his great collections: Schloss Ambras, built during the 16th century for Archduke Ferdinand II and his wife Philippine Welser.
Above right: Gallery of Gods, grimaces and mythical creatures: the terracotta figures in the inner courtyard of Schloss Schallaburg, Lower Austria.
Below: One of the most beautiful Renaissance rooms in Europe: the Spanish Hall in Schloss Ambras, framed by 27 full-figure portraits of the Tyrolean sovereigns.

Above left: Mighty old beamed ceiling: the Rittersaal in the Rosenburg Castle, Lower Austria.
Above right: The ceiling fresco by Josef Ferdinand Fromiller in the Großer Wappensaal of the Klagenfurt Landhaus.
Below left: Original decoration of the late-Gothic Fürstenzimmer with twisted marble columns: the "Golden Room" in the Fortress Hohensalzburg.
Below right: Gothic winding staircase in Schloss Pöggstall in the Waldviertel.
Opposite page: Monument of constant self-confidence: 650 coats of arms decorate the walls designed by Josef Ferdinand Fromiller of the Großer Wappensaal in Klagenfurt.

Following double page: Fascinating palace structure of unrivalled harmony and a Habsburg place of remembrance: Schloss Schönbrunn, built between 1695 and 1711 based on designs by Johann Bernhard Fischer von Erlach.

Above: View from the naiad fountain, a work by Christian Wilhelm Beyers, at the front of the garden in Schloss Schönbrunn.

Opposite page
Above: The Große Galerie, the glamorous centre point of the state rooms in Schönbrunn, with ceiling frescos by Gregorio Guglielmi.
Below left: The Rösselzimmer with Marschal table at which the highest military and officers of the court dined.
Below right: Remembrance room for Emperor Franz I Stephan, Maria Theresia's husband: the Vieux-Laque room with black lacquered tables from Beijing.

Above left: Artistic lead cast: Original figure of the Providentia Fountain on the Neuer Markt by Georg Raphael Donner in the Marbel Room of the Lower Belvedere.
Above right: Grey stone sphinxes watch over the staircase in the atmospheric gardens.
Below left: The summer residence of the war hero Prince Eugene is also the memorial to the Second Republic: On 15 May 1955 the Austrian state treaty was signed here.
Below right: In the Mirror Cabinet in the Lower Belvedere: Apotheosis of Prince Eugene by Balthasar Permoser, 1721.

Opposite page: A Baroque *gesamtkunstwerk*: The Belvedere, the summer residence of Prince Eugene, built between 1720 and 1723 based on designs by Johann Lukas von Hildebrandt.

Above: The heart of ancient Salzburg: Residence and cathedral; left, the Franciscan church.

Opposite page
Below left: Never conquered: the Fortress Hohensalzburg, the emblem of the Mozart city, seen from the Capuchin abbey.
Below right: Huge former fortress above the Salzachtal valley: Fortress Hohenwerfen, first mentioned in documents in the year 1139.

Above: The double-headed eagle above the main entrance to the Neue Burg.
Below: Renaissance portal in the Hofburg: the Schweizertor (1552/53). The balls for the chains of the draw bridge are a reminder of the former Medieval fortress.

Left: Vienna's world in the shadow of the Habsburg double-headed eagle: Heldenplatz, Neue Burg and Neue Burgtor (right); in the foreground the Theseus Temple.

Above: Symbolising the universalness of knowledge: the grand State Hall in the Austrian National Library with ceiling frescoes by Daniel Gran, built between 1723 and 1726 by Joseph Emanuel Fischer von Erlach based on designs of his father, Johann Bernhard.

Opposite page
Above left: Allegories of persistence and strength carrying the atlas: Figurenschmuck by Lorenzo Mattielli over the gable of the former civic armoury on Platz Am Hof.
Above right: The Austrian war hero par excellence: Monument of Prince Eugene of Savoy on Heldenplatz.
Below: In the arcades of the Stallburg the Lipizzaner horses enjoy their view. The training of the young stallions for the Spanish Riding School takes at least five years.

Above: An Otto Wagner masterpiece and emblem of the Viennese modern: the St. Leopold's church, Am Steinhof, built between 1904 and 1907. The cupola is covered with gilded copperplate.
Below left: Jugendstilhaus by Otto Wagner on the Linke Wienzeile, built in 1898/99, with reliefs by Kolo Moser.
Below right: the exhibition building of the Secession by Josef Maria Olbrich, built in 1897/98, became the symbol for the departure of Viennese art at the turn of the century.

Following double page: View from Vienna City Hall to the inner city. In the foreground the Ringstrase with the Burgtheater, the second-oldest surviving theatre in Europe.

In the name of Jugendstil: the high altar of St. Leopold's church with mosaics by Leopold Forster designed by Remigius Geyling.

MYTHS &
MEMORIES

Even if spiteful critics maintain otherwise from time to time, Austria is a modern, globally networked industrial country, which has worked hard for its prosperity. It is a country that is open to new technological innovations. In some areas, such as climate and environmental protection, Austrian businesses are pace-setters in international development. But Austria is successful on more than just an economic level: This "bigger" Austria is a fascinating place of remembrance in Europe, an overflowing reservoir of myths and narratives full of exemplary reflections of occidental history.

Those simply traversing Austria's cultural landscapes on the grey concrete of the motorways won't be able to discover the magic of this country. But if you enter the quiet worlds on the other side of the traffic noise and activity, if you are patient and engage in the narratives of our forefathers, the myths and legends, you will discover the secret fortune of Austria, a second reality, fantastic and touching where the past of a country will inspire new life. Strange monstrosities, lindworms and basilisks emerge from the depths of time, the powers of heaven and hell, ghosts and demons. The gods of the Celts live on in fairies and white women, in rebellious devils, ugly water sprites and seductive nixes. Prey-hungry robber barons and noble crusaders cavorted on proud castles; ladies and men of the manor, monks and nuns, farmers and handymen fought for their happiness.

They are stories of hope and justice in which the bad are punished and the good are rewarded. They are stories of war and peace, of desperate revolts against oppression and exploitation; of natural catastrophes, starvation and plagues. The trauma of the bloody Turkish wars finds its voice here as does the downfall of the Templar Knights or the heroic tales of the battle against Napoleon Bonaparte's *grande armée*. The focal points of these myths have become national memorials in many cases; heroic places that are testimony to Austrian mythology. For example the Tyroleans' "Heldenberg", the Bergisel hill in southern Innsbruck, where in 1809 the Tyrolean "freedom fighters" under their legendary commander Andreas Hofer defeated the French and the Bavarians in four battles. And the Kahlenberg in Vienna, today a favourite destination of the Viennese: This is where, on the early morning of 12 September 1683, ordered by Poland's King Jan III Sobieski, the memorable attack of the allied forces on the Turkish troupes around Vienna began, which led to the huge change in the battle against the Ottomans. A commemorative plaque on St. Josef's church refers to this event that was of major world-historical importance.

Another place that played a particular fateful role in Austria is the small Wienerwald municipality of Mayerling. The hunting lodge situated here was the where the Austrian heir to the throne Archduke Rudolf shot his 17-year-old lover Mary Freiin von Vetsera and then himself on the eve of 29 January 1889 under mysterious circumstances. A Habsburg family drama that became the beacon of the downfall of the monarchy.

And in Vienna, stepping out from under the low vaults of the Inner Burgtor to the large, bright Heldenplatz it is almost impossible not to think about 15 March 1938, when the insane Führer Adolf Hitler announced the "biggest confirmation of operation" of his life from the balcony of the Neue Hofburg, Austria's annexation to the national socialist German Empire.

One of the biggest semi-myths in Austrian "national mythology" is not least the ever-circulated story of Austria as a music country. Even if music is not necessarily born from Austria's

Opposite page: The empire of the Habsburgers was lost; the yellow-black double-headed eagle remained: Entrance on the main square of Stockerau, Lower Austria.

landscape as some enthusiasts like to maintain, it does enjoy a particular significance. Music became the key symbol for ease and the lust for life of the Austrian people. If you believe the sources, the delight in musical entertainment pulsated in the veins of the Austrian states as early as the Middle Ages; its further development is closely connected to the love that the Habsburg rulers had to musical art. With the foundation of the Viennese *Hofmusikkapelle*, Emperor Maximilian I set the first standard. With the rise of the Baroque opera, the imperial residence in Vienna became even more popular and attractive. Numerous composers, mainly from Italy, found a new home at the court. Their works were enthusiastically embraced. Alongside the ruling house, the Austrian high nobility also distinguished itself as supporters of music. Joseph Haydn, creator of the early classical symphony and the classic string quartets, was head of Count Esterházy's *musikkapelle* in Eisenstadt; Ludwig van Beethoven, suffering increasingly from loss of hearing, was patronized by Count Lobkowitz. The wunderkind Wolfgang Amadeus Mozart, the musical genius par excellence, born in Salzburg and spent years travelling throughout Europe, then found a new home as royal "court composer" in the Imperial city, where his immortal works such as *The Marriage of Figaro* and *The Magic Flute* were composed.

While Beethoven and Franz Schubert, the youngest of the Viennese classicists, were still working on their magnificent compositions, new, intoxicating light music was conquering the dance halls of the Danube metropolis: the waltz. Criticised as being "immoral" by grumpy contemporaries, the spirited new dance was enthusiastically embraced by the public. The waltz melodies by Johann Strauss son, the "Waltz King", above all the *Blue Danube Waltz*, conquered the world. Since then, Austria and waltzes have become culturally synonymous. And when listening very carefully to this music, you may discover something "typically Austrian". In the soft "sound waves" of the waltz you won't only hear joviality and lust for life but also a touch of melancholy, born of the knowledge of the transience of happiness, from the great sentimental question of unknown eternity.

Right: A monument to a lost working world: old mills and saws in Schöllbüchl an der Lainsitz near Weitra.

Above left: Lonely blocks of granite in the Waldviertel are testimony to unimaginably distant times: the camel rock in Schmerbach.
Below left: The stony "guard" in Bruderndorf.
Right: Stone memorial, lest we forget: column shrine in Bruderndorf on the street to Langschlag.

Opposite page: Sign posts announcing the life and faith of people, their hope and connection to God: late-Gothic tabernacle column shrine north of Thail in Groß Gerungs.

Above: The landmark of Klagenfurt shrouded in myths: the Lindworm fountain, built in 1624 commissioned by the Carinthian estates of the country.
Below left: Air paintings on the facade of a former pub in the old mining town of Kössen, Tyrol.
Below right: Flag-holding landsknechte: Fähnrichstor at Burg Hochosterwitz castle, Carinthia.

Opposite page: Commissioned by Emperor Maximilian I in memory of the turn of the century at 1500: the golden roof in Innsbruck.

Above left: Ubiquitous double-headed eagle: under the roof ridge of the former mail station of Maissau, Lower Austria.
Above right: On the wooden Renaissance door, Preuenhueberhaus in Weyer an der Enns, Upper Austria.
Below: Above the shop door of the court bakery Edegger-Tax in Hofgasse, Graz.

Opposite page: Emperor Franz Joseph I, a passionate hunter, rules over the fountain on the Radmer main square, Styria.

Above left: In the Capuchin crypt, the mausoleum of the Habsburgs: the magnificent double sarcophagus of Emperor Franz I Stephan and his wife Maria Theresia.
Above right: The members of the royal family will always exist with their hearts in the church: the "Herzgrüfterl – *heart crypt*" in Loretto Chapel, Augustinerkirche.
Below left: The most important symbol of rule of ancient Europe: the crown of the Holy Roman Empire, 10th century. The Treasury in the Hofburg.
Below right: The Austrian imperial crown, a family crown of Rudolf II from the 16th century.

The dream couple of the 19th century: Emperor Franz Joseph I and Empress Elisabeth, called "Sisi". Two paintings by Franz Xaver Winterhalter from 1865. Franz Joseph is wearing a gala uniform, Elisabeth with the famous diamonds in her hair.

Above: World famous tradition: the annual New Year's concert given by the Vienna Philharmonic in the Golden Hall of the Vienna Musikverein.

Opposite page: A legendary ambassador of Viennese music and lust for life: The "Waltz King" Johann Strauss. Monument by Edmund Hellmer in Stadtpark, Vienna.

Following double page: Sign post for half a millennium: the "twisted cross" west of Zwettl Abbey, built in the year 1500 by Abbot Wolfgang II Örtel.

A LAND OF
WELL-BEING

Austria is not a large country but it has weight, if it's about enjoying the beautiful sides of life and absorbing renewed energy for the tasks of the every day. It is a country full of places of happiness and of power, a stronghold of quality of life in the heart of Europe. Those who need a break, need to slow down or are looking for recuperation from unrelenting pace and hectic, can hope that their needs will be met here. A true "power place" on the Continent, Austria doesn't only allow an encounter with the treasures of historical, museum-like Europe, but also fantastic, energy and harmony-giving landscapes. It is an Eldorado for the friend of nature hungry for discovery and adventure who prefers to move away from the tourist centres. A paradise for skiing enthusiasts and mountain climbers and hikers and mountain bikers, for everyone wanting to go their own way and look for repose of their own accord – eye to eye with nature, free and independent. For people who want to go beyond their borders and experience new things, for those who want that "kick", that moment where control over danger and risk, triumphing over fatigue and weakness, becomes an experience to be relished. No rock face is too steep, no ski slope too difficult, no gorge too narrow. The possibilities of experiencing nature are endless. No other European country has such a high number of marked hiking trails as Austria – from the classic pilgrimage trails to the European Marian sanctuary Mariazell to spectacular long hiking trails; challenging mountain hikes for top-fit passionate hikers to comfortable family hikes. Since the Heiligenblut Agreement, in which the states Tyrol, Salzburg and Carinthia agreed on the formation of the first Austrian National Park in 1971, seven national parks were formed to date in the name of the protection of unique landscapes: the national parks Hohe Tauern and Neusiedler See – Seewinkel (together with Hungary's national park Fertö-Hanság), the national park Donau-Auen, Kalkalpen National Park in the Upper Austrian pre-alps, Thayatal National Park (in conjunction with the Czech Republic's Podyjí National Park) and Gesäuse National Park in Upper Styria and Nockberge mountains in the western part of the Gurktal Alps in Carinthia (ranked as "protected areas" by the International Union for the Conservation of Nature). In addition, since 1962, 41 parks have been created with a total area of 305,000 hectares: from Blockheide Eibenstein-Gmünd in the Waldviertel to the Dobratsch; from Geschriebenstein in Burgenland, the eastern foothills of the Alps at the Austrian-Hungarian border to the Zillertal Alps in Tyrol. This is supposed to facilitate the upkeep of ancient cultural landscapes in their native splendour and be open to visitors.

In summer and autumn of 1836 when the extravagant English Lady Frances Trollope travelled through Austria and then stopped in Vienna for some months, she had the impression that the Austrians literally were "replete with happiness". The country was one without troubles; the propensity for amusement traversed all classes of society equally. The days of the "always merry" savourers which Trollope and other visitors to the Habsburg monarchy so enthusiastically speak of have in the meantime passed. Also in Vienna, the city in which the Frenchman Victor Tissot still in 1878 said that one couldn't find more amusement, even in paradise.

Life may no longer be a constant party, but the red-white-red areas of basic lust for life still exist, where physical and mental well-being is still catered to. For example, the many pubs or taverns, where for a long time now great food and drinks are served, where you can sit with friends and acquaintances comfortably and forget the burdens of the every day. There are the idyllic wine taverns with their excellent home-made wines and

Opposite page: A farmhouse window in Haslach, Mühlviertel.

the legendary coffee houses, which above all in Vienna sill maintain the ancient Austrian coffee house culture – a relaxed, stylish world of enjoyment in which time often seems to stop. Gourmets will find Austria to be a veritable land of plenty. The spectrum of culinary delicacies begins with the classics of old-Austrian, Viennese cuisine – Wiener Schnitzel, Tafelspitz, roasted chicken, Beuschel, goulash, Kaiserschmarren, apple strudel and gugelhupf – to the perfectly composed treats in the temples of exquisite top-class cuisine. This unequalled range is not least made possible by the produce of Austrian farmers, who make sure that the chefs are provided with first-class, healthy and good-tasting products. Be it fine lamb, game and fish dishes or those made with asparagus, mushrooms and potatoes; Salzburger Nockerl or Kärntner Kasnudeln, Tiroler Gröstl or Upper Austrian knödel cuisine, Kärntner Reindling or the classics of the Austrian torte world, the Sacher Torte – each individual culinary landscape of Austria has developed its own wonderful specialities.

As sacrificially as the Austrian cooks produce their wares, the winegrowers of the country also deliver. As documents show, viniculture is older than Austria and was already being practiced in the time of the Celts. The Romans continued to cultivate wine: Emperor Probus lifted the ban on the growing of vines and thus the first vineyards emerged at the eastern edge of the Wienerwald, along the so-called "thermal line", and around the Neusiedler See. In the meantime, Austrian wine has an excellent reputation worldwide; Top wines from the Wachau region, from southern Styria or the hills around the Neusiedler See don't need to be afraid of international comparisons. A great deal of love and sensitivity from the winemakers goes into making a good drop. And what could be nicer than to open a bottle of wine at a tasting in a companionable environment, to toast with a hearty "Cheers!" and to enjoy a moment of cheerfulness and peace?

Right: Dream landscape for the soul: Lake Constance and Bregenz Bay, with the snow-capped Alp peaks in the background.

Above: Sunny holiday paradise with Mediterranean flair: Wörthersee Lake in Carinthia.

Opposite page
Above: The Pannonian steppe lake in the east: Ships on the Neusiedler See Lake.
Below left: Favourite visiting place in the Waldviertel: the Ottenstein reservoir with the Lichtenfel ruins.
Below right: One of the warmest bathing lakes in the Alps: the idyllic Schwarzsee Lake between Reith and Kitzbühel, Tyrol.

Above: Departing point and destination for many a hiking path and pilgrimage: the pilgrimage church Frauenberg bei Admont; the peaks of the Hochtorgruppe mountains in the Ennstal Alps.

Opposite page: Once a dreamy Rhaeto-Romanic mountain village, today a popular winter sports destination: Fiss in the so-called "Oberen Gericht" region of Tyrol.

Above left: Water and rocks unite in a unique landscape in the Salzkammergut: Sunset on the Attersee Lake.
Above right: One of the oldest buildings in the Salzkammergut: Schloss Ort on the Traunsee Lake; owned by the Habsburgs until 1918.
Below: Genuine, up-kept custom: performers in national costume on the Grundlsee Lake in the Styrian Salzkammergut.

Idyll on the Hallstätter See Lake: View from the boat house to the Catholic parish church of Hallstatt.

The order of the old world is still preserved in some places: row of houses on the Main Square of Drosendorf an der Thaya, Lower Austria.

A journey into Austria's culinary diversity: pumpkin harvest in south-eastern Styria; apples from the Mostviertel; Family Kollwentz's wine cellars in Großhöflein, Burgenland; at the Schilcher winery Knappitsch in Wernersdorf, western Styria; afternoon tea in a wine tavern; mushrooms from the Waldviertel.

Above left: Paradise of fun: a rollercoaster at the Vienna Prater.
Above right: Classic Viennese coffeehouse culture: the artists' café Hawelka.
Below left: Celebration on the water with beer: kermesse in Langschlag, Lower Austria.
Below right: Promising relaxation in a convivial atmosphere: a wine tavern in Probusgasse in Heiligenstadt, Vienna.

Above: Meeting place for young and old: MuseumsQuartier Wien connects revitalized imperial architecture with modern exhibition spaces.

Following double page: Arcadia north of the Alps: landscape on the southern Styrian wine trail.

AUSTRIA THROUGH TIME

Ca. 300,000–26,000 BC: Numerous cave findings document the first traces of human life on current Austrian territory.

3,900–2,300/2,200 BC: Stilt houses in the Salzkammergut and on Lake Constance. Most important finding: the "Ötzi" a glacial mummy from 3,400 BC, found on the Hauslabjoch mountain in the Ötztal Alps.

400 BC – 1 AD: Early Iron Age (La Tène Age). The Celts penetrate the Austrian realm.

Around 15 BC: Roman occupation of Noricum and surrender of Rhaetia. Consequently, the provinces Rhaetia, Noricum and Pannonia are established.

304 AD: Persecution of the Christians under Emperor Diocletian. Martyrdom of St. Florian in Lauriacum/Enns.

791/803: Charles the Great ruins the Avar state. Carolingian Mark is established.

4 July 907: Defeat of a Bavarian army at Pressburg against the Hungarians – end of the Carolingian Mark.

10 August 955: Battle of Lechfeld at Augsburg. Otto I conquers the Hungarians. The region east of the Enns and west of the Wienerwald again falls to Bavarian rule as the 'Ottonian Mark'.

976: Beginning of the Babenberg rule: Emperor Otto II enfeoffs Leopold I with the margraviate between Enns and Traisen.

1 November 996: First written documentation of the name "Ostarrîchi".

8 September 1156: *Privilegium minus:* Austria is elevated to a duchy.

17 August 1186: Georgenberg Pact: The childless Duke Ottakar IV of Styria instates Duke Leopold V as heir. With his death in1192, Styria goes to the Babenbergs.

15 June 1246: With the death of Duke Frederick II the Quarrelsome in the battle at the Leitha river against Hungary, the rule of the Babenbergs ends.

1251/52: Przemysl Ottokar II of Bohemia occupies the Babenberg territories.

26 August 1278: King Rudolf I is victorious in the battle at Dürnkrut and Jedenspeigen over Przemysl Ottokar, who dies in battle. The Habsburg rule in Austria begins.

1335: Carinthia, South Tyrol and Carniola are enfeoffed to the Habsburgs.

1358/59: *Privilegium Maius:* As a reaction to the Golden Bull (1356), Duke Rudolf IV the Founder, has this document faked to empower Austria.

Opposite page: Magical old Vienna: Griechengasse, named after the Levantine business people who once lived here.

26 January 1363: Countess Margaret Maultasch assigns the rule of Tyrol to Rudolf IV.

1375: Large parts of today's Vorarlberg fall into Austrian ownership.

6 July 1415: Conviction and burning of Jan Hus in Constance. The Hussite Wars begin (until about 1436).

1420: Beginning of the persecution of the Jews in Vienna (Vienna Geserah) and Enns.

21 October 1496: The Habsburgs' "Spanish marriages": Philip the Handsome, one of Maximilian I's sons, marries Joanna of Castile-Aragon. In 1497 Maximilian's daughter Margaret marries Juan of Spain, Joanna's brother.

22 July 1515: Double wedding of the Habsburg und Jagiellon aspirants to the throne in St. Stephen's cathedral: Emperor Maximilian's grand-daughter Maria marries Louis of Hungary; Maria's brother Archduke Ferdinand takes Anna, the daughter of King Vladislas II, as his wife.

29 August 1526: Battle of Mohács – The Turks are victorious over the Hungarians; King Ludwig dies in battle. Hungary and Bohemia fall to House of Habsburg rule.

25 September until 14 October 1529: First Turkish occupation of Vienna by Sultan Süleiman the Magnificent.

1595/97: Peasant revolt in Upper and Lower Austria.

1618 – 1648: The Thirty Years' War. Northern Lower Austria and Vorarlberg suffer most under the sieges.

1626: Revolt of the Upper Austrian peasants led by Stefan Fadinger.

1 August 1664: Battle of Mogersdorf an der Raab. First victory against the Turks on an open field battle under Raimund Count Montecuccoli.

1679: Major plague epidemic in Austria.

14 July – 12 September 1683: Second Turkish occupation of Vienna. Grand Vizier Kara Mustafa succumbs to the allies in the decisive battle.

26 January 1699: Treaty of Karlowitz. The Ottoman Empire is forced to cede Hungary and Siebenbürgen to Austria.

1701 – 1714: Spanish War of Succession.

19 April 1713: Pragmatic Sanction: Emperor Charles VI declares his daughter as heiress and at the same time decrees that the Habsburg realm cannot be divided.

1740 – 1748: Maria Theresia defends her inheritance against Prussia and Bavaria; she is unable to hinder the loss of Silesia.

1756 – 1763: Seven Year War between Austria and Prussia.

5 August 1772: First division of Poland.

Galicia and Lodomeria fall to Austria.

1775: Occupation of Bukovina by Austrian troupes.

1778 – 1779: Bavarian War of Succession. The Innviertel falls to Austria.

24 October 1795: Third division of Poland. Austria receives East Galicia to Bug.

11 August 1804: As Franz I, Franz II takes the title of "Emperor of Austria".

6 August 1806: End of the Holy Roman Empire: Franz I renounces the title of Roman Emperor.

1809: Austria goes to war against Napoleon. Archduke Charles wins the battle at Aspern (21/22 May), but loses the decisive battle at Deutsch-Wagram (6/7 July). The victories of the Tyrolean peasants under Andreas Hofer on the Bergisel hill are in vain.

September 1814 – June 1815: Vienna Congress: The reorganisation of Europe is determined.

1 May 1816: Salzburg is officially ceded to Austria.

13 March 1848: Revolution breaks out in Vienna; State Chancellor Count Metternich steps down.

31 October 1848: Revolutionary Vienna is taken by imperial troupes.

2 December 1848: Franz Joseph I ascends to the throne at 18 years of age.

24 April 1854: Emperor Franz Joseph I marries Princess Elisabeth in Bavaria ('Sisi').

24 June 1859: Battle of Solferino. Austria relinquishes Lombardy to France and the kingdom of Sardinia.

1866: War against the Prussians. Heavy losses in the Battle of Königgrätz – Venetia is ceded to Italy.

15 March 1867: "Compromise" with Hungary. Beginning of the dual monarchy.

21 April 1879: Austria-Hungary occupies Bosnia and Herzegovina.

30 January 1889: Habsburg family drama in Mayerling: Crown Prince Rudolf shoots Mary Vetsera and then himself.

14 – 24 May 1907: General elections are held in Austria for the first time.

5 October 1908: Annexation of Bosnia-Herzegovina.

28 June 1914: Murder of the heir to the throne Archduke Ferdinand in Sarajevo.

28 July 1914: Austria-Hungary declare war on Serbia. Beginning of World War I.

21 November 1916: Death of Emperor Franz Joseph I; he is succeeded by Emperor Charles I

3/4 November 1918: Armistice between Austria-Hungary and the Allies.

11 November 1918: Emperor Charles I relinquishes participation in the administration of the State.

12 November 1918: The democratic

Republic "Germany-Austria" is proclaimed.

10 September 1919: The Saint-Germain-en-Laye state treaty is signed.

10 October 1920: Referendum in Carinthia: Nearly the whole Slovenian part of Carinthia votes for Austria.

14 – 16 December 1921: Referendum in western Hungary. Burgenland becomes part of Austria.

12 – 15 February 1934: Civil war in Austria.

25 July 1934: National Socialist rebels murder State Chancellor Engelbert Dollfuß. He is succeeded by Kurt Schuschnigg.

12 March 1938: The Anschluss. German armed forces march into Austria.

15 March 1938: The Führer gives a speech at the Vienna Heldenplatz.

10 April 1938: Referendum about Austria's Anschluss to the German Empire; 99.73 % of voters vote 'yes'.

1 September 1939: Beginning of World War II. Hundreds of thousands of Austrians die on the battlefields for the Führer.

30 October/1 November 1943: Moscow Declaration. The Allies call for the establishment of a free Austria.

27 April 1945: The Second Republic is proclaimed and a provisional government under Karl Renner is established.

4 July 1945: The occupation zones of the four victorious powers are established.

25 November 1945: The first elections in the Second Republic result in an absolute majority of the Austrian Peoples' Party (ÖVP); Leopold Figl becomes federal chancellor.

15 May 1955: The Austrian State Treaty is signed.

26 October 1955: The national parliament determines the federal law about Austria's perpetual neutrality.

15 December 1955: Austria becomes a member of UNO.

23 October 1956: Beginning of the Hungarian revolt; Austria takes on over 100,000 refugees.

21 April 1970: Change of power and the beginning of a new political era: Bruno Kreisky (SPÖ – Social Democrats) builds a social-democratic minority.

27 June 1989: Fall of the Iron Curtain: Foreign Minister Alois Mock and his Hungarian counterpart Gyula Horn cut through the barbed wire fence at Klingenbach.

12 June 1994: Referendum about Austria's admission to the European Union.

24 June 1994: EU ascension treaty is signed on Corfu.

1 January 1995: Austria becomes a member of the European Union.

1 January 2006 – 30 June 2006: Austria's second EU presidency.

Header page: Daybreak in the Inntal valley: the pilgrimage Church in Arzl east of Innsbruck.
Trailer page: Land on the vast river: View from Braunsberg to the Danube.

The photographer

Gerhard Trumler, born in 1937 in Vienna. Has worked as a freelance photographer since 1969. He lives with his family in Vienna and in Fraberg in the Waldviertel.
Since 1978 Gerhard Trumler has published over 130 books; numerous awards won.

The author

Johannes Sachslehner, born in 1957 in Scheibbs, Doctor of Philosophy.
Author of numerous non-fiction books on historical and art-historical subjects.

Photos

Photo: Assam: 99
© Alp Line, St. Johann in Tyrol: 96/97
Willfried Gredler-Oxenbauer: 71 above and below right, 73 right above and below,
    88 below (left and right, © Art History Museum Vienna),
    89 (left and right, © Art History Museum Vienna)
Robert Bouchal: 46 below
Collections from the Augustine monastery Klosterneuburg: 16
Natural History Museum Vienna: 19 above left (Photo: Gerhard Trumler)
Höbarthmuseum, Horn: 19 below right (Photo: Gerhard Trumler)

All other photos are originals by Gerhard Trumler.

ISBN 978-3-85431-485-1

© 2009 by Pichler Verlag in der Verlagsgruppe Styria GmbH & Co KG
Vienna-Graz-Klagenfurt
All rights reserved
www.pichlerverlag.at

Translation: Mý Huê McGowran

Cover design: Bruno Wegscheider
Book design and production: Franz Hanns
Reproduction: Pixelstorm, Vienna
Printing and binding: Druckerei Theiss GmbH, St. Stefan im Lavanttal